BREATH OF LIGHT

BREATH OF LIGHT

JUSTIN BAKER

To order additional copies of this book, contact:
Xlibris
1-800-455-039
www.Xlibris.com.au
Orders@Xlibris.com.au
698455

CONTENTS

*"There's a hole in the bucket, dear Liza dear Liza there's a hole in the bucket, dear Liza a hole."

"We'll fix it, dear Henry dear Henry dear Henry well fix it, dear Henry dear Henry fix it."

"With what shall I fix it? Dear Liza dear Liza, with what shall I fix it dear Liza with what?

(*Taken from part of an old English Nursery Rhyme)

"INTRODUCTION"

The "Breath of Light" is a breath cultivation technique that works with the body's own Bio-Mechanics, and internal circuitry.

Those familiar with Chi Gung, Tantra or other such practices, may recognise some similarities, with this practice. This is because the body's internal Bio-Mechanical workings are one and the same.

The Balancing of Solar [Male] and Lunar [female] energies are a prerequisite to Raising the Kundalini, [the energy that rises up the centre of the spine, when balance is attained], no matter what school of thought, you are coming from.

The raising of the Kundalini, and the ability to Give, Universal Life force Energies, from within us, to all that surrounds us, on a daily basis, is all of our Hidden potential.

'Enlightenment is our Destiny!'

Most of us spend our entire life, working at 5% of our Energetic Potential, and using 5% of our brain cells etc. It's time we taped into the other 95%. For too long, the Secret of our Hidden Potential has been kept by secret brotherhoods, and those in powerful positions.

WE were made in Gods Likeness, and can be a Source of Bio-Photonic Light, and pure Universal Life-force Energy to all that surrounds us, just like a Star, to our own universe.

We are all potentially, Sun Gods! And all that is required to experience this is the <u>true balancing </u>of our body's Energy Centres. Balance equals spontaneous Enlightenment.

It does not matter what path in life you choose to walk, you will be breathing as you walk that path, and those very breaths can be cultivated simultaneously with any activity at all. Even other cultivation methods based on stance and movements, such as are found in Taoism, Etc.

The practice of the "Breath of Light" teaches us how to switch <u>on,</u> and tap into, the other 95% of our brain and energetic output potential. It teaches us how to switch on the body's Central Circuit, and how to cultivate Solar and Lunar energies, to attain the Balance of all the body's Chakras [energy centres]. This will result in spontaneous Enlightenment, <u>if you are enduring in your daily practice.</u>

'This is a form of internal Alchemy.' Designed to balance all the body's Chakras and raise the Kundalini. When balance is attained, our body becomes a kind of Bio-Photonic Light and Life Force Generator or Star. With the practice of the "Breath of Light" there are no limits to the amount of energy we can give, to all that's around us, on a continual basis.

As a younger man I was amazed how there could be workings within my own body, that I was unaware of. When I discovered, "Çoitus Interruptus"

The ability of a man to use inner muscle contractions, namely the perineum muscles, to control and direct the flow of ejaculation within us, as we Orgasm. Redirecting its flow into the sacral chamber, [that holds a pool of seminal fluid, that circulates throughout our spine and up around our brain as protective fluid]. We can hold on to our ejaculation and Energy usually lost, and still have a great orgasm. This fluid then nourishes our spine and brain from within with valuable nutrients, and the energies are not lost, or thrown away.

If a man chooses to follow the advice of the Tantric masters, he can retain every ejaculation not intended for reproduction. One third of a man's daily energy is in that little amount of fluid, so 'Hold On To It', and gain that otherwise lost energy with each Orgasm.

"So how is it done?"

With quick contractions of the perineum and anus muscles, as fast as we possibly can, as we orgasm!

[Or]

We can also manually press with our fingers, half way along the coitus, between the testicles and the anus. This is more for beginners who have not mastered the muscle control method, which is better, as you are not trying to locate the right pressure point, as you're enjoying your orgasm. 'Practice makes perfect'

For a more detailed explanation of this method, please check out, [Mantak Chia's Book, Taoist Secrets of Love, Cultivating Male Sexual Energy.]

Most people are unaware of their hidden potential, and all that is stoping us from experiencing it, is not being Balanced.

The Breath of Light Technique is designed to bring us into a natural state of balance, allowing the Kundalini to rise with no more than the thought, of doing so. It allows us to Attain and Maintain Balance, throughout our daily lives, regardless of what activities we are doing.

Our potential is truly amazing; we can be true Co-Creators and a source, of both Life Force and Bio-photonic Light, each and every day of our lives. [Instead of competing to be the point of others attention, to receive energy]

We are potentially, Sun gods and Goddesses! It is written, "We were made in Gods likeness, and its true!". And as if that's not amazing enough, we can do this at Will, with the Harmony of our Mind, Body and Spirit and the true Balancing of our body's energetic system.

This Technique, coupled with Conscious Awareness is a wonderful daily spiritual discipline. I am leading you to the 'spring of life', but it's up to you to drink.

Just like the Gnostic way of teaching, you will learn from your direct experience with the Holy Spirit, and its production from within you, as a direct result of your "breath of Light" practice.

But with practice, this technique transforms from being a technique, becoming a natural way of controlling the flow of energy's within us as we naturally breathe. We Wilfully Balance, Solar and Lunar Energy's within us to create Universal Life Force Energy's [Kundalini or Holy Spirit] from our Core star and centre of gravity. This energy rises up from our base chakra, right through the centre of our spine, and out of our heart and crown chakras, just like a fountain.

In order to achieve this, we work with an important,[but little known about] Circuit, that runs right through the centre of our body's, and through all of the body's major energy centres.

With this form of Breath Cultivation, we collect Solar and Lunar energy's within this important 'Central Circuit', as we naturally breathe. Collecting and combining them within, until balance is attained, and we create universal life force energy as a direct result of their unity. With balance 'Enlightenment is Spontaneous.'

"The Breath of Light" Is a three step technique, we add to our natural breath cycle. Using more of the body's muscles as we breathe, to control the flow of Solar Energy [coming through the crown chakra from the heavens above with each inward breath] and Lunar Energy [coming through the root chakra, from the earth below, with each outward breath].

95% of the energy's flowing through us are lost with each breath, unless we make the effort to hold on to them, by using internal contractions of the perineum, and torso alternately, with each in and outward breath.

Just as the heart pumps and relaxes, continually. So it is with the "Breath of Light" technique. We pump and relax these two different muscle groups with the in and outward breath.

At first you may choose to add the "Breath of Light" to your meditation practice and experiment with the energy's you experience within, but know this! With practice every breath can be cultivated, and utilised for your Spiritual Development. Every breath can be utilized to bring daily Balance, and directly raise your vibrational level, allowing spontaneous Enlightenment to occur.

We tend to take slower, deeper and more conscious, breaths while practicing the "Breath of light". We strengthen a variety of muscles and glands, weak in most people, and awaken dormant brain cells, by driving fresh energy into the brain and the body's 'Central Circuit', with each and every breath.

Have you ever wondered how to turn on the other 95% of your brain cells? Well why not start feeding them with energy, with this daily spiritual practice. Your tongue is the Master switch of your body's Central Circuit. Start training it to remain connected to the point; you can feel as a lump just back from the highest part of your upper palate. We place the tip of our tongue to the middle of that lumpy bit, and this sends energy directly through your pituitary gland, and the brain, and switches ON, the Central Circuit which flows through all of the body's energy centres.

"This is a physical path, to spiritual success."

Most of us spend our whole life out of balance, without even knowing it. Only after a powerful initiation experience, I came to discover my own potential as a human being, and experienced how we can be sources, of Bio-Photonic Light, and universal Life Force Energy's, to all that surrounds us. But it took me two years, to discover how I could reproduce the initiatory experience, and the power of the Holy Spirit, that comes from the centre of our body, from our Core star, by my own Will and doing. And now if you are open to it, I am going to share that Knowledge, with you. But remember this,' knowledge not put into practice, is sterile.'

Enlightenment is a Natural, State of Being, when Balance is attained. It's the Birthright, of every human being, to give Birth to Universal Life Force Energy's from within us without limit, 'Just like a sun'. "The Breath of Light" is an internal, Alchemy designed to bring whoever practices it, into balance, provided they are persistent and enduring with their practice.

[CHAPTER ONE]

"IGNORANCE IS NOT BLISS"

The "Breath of Light" is a Breath Cultivation Technique. Aiming at Balancing, the body's internal energy's within the body's Central Circuit, allowing the Kundalini to rise up from the base chakra, up through the heart and crown chakras like a fountain.

It's a Daily Spiritual Discipline, of the highest order, on the path to continual, Enlightenment. It requires great discipline to Master, but the rewards are priceless, and well worth the effort. Most people live there entire life, using 5% of their brain and energetic output potential.

There are many reasons to practice this wonderful daily spiritual discipline, which offers the practitioner, clear benefits, such as strengthening various Glands and Muscles in the body, as well as an impressive increase in our energy levels that we can channel into any activity we are involved in.

Our body's can in fact produce, limitless amounts of Universal Life Force Energy, and Bio-Photonic Light, on a daily basis, as long as we maintain Balance with the practice of "The Breath of Light".

The Budda who found Enlightenment under the Bodhi Tree, is said to have taught those disciples close to him, to practice a form of Breath Cultivation, and many of his disciples experienced Enlightenment for them self's, as a direct result of their daily "Cultivation Practice".

It is known that Jesus travelled to the Himalayas in the younger years of his life, before the age of 30 years old, and He studied the Buddhist school of thought, and Mastered it.

There is a Library called the "Himundi Library" in the Himalayas. It is run by Buddhist Monks, and they have records on scrolls that are kept deep down in underground caverns. These records go back thousands of years. And they say, he was there !

The "Breath of Light" shows us how to switch ON and utilize the body's Central Circuit. We Cultivate Solar [Male] and Lunar [Female] Energy's inside this important, Circuit which we use as a kind, of vessel to contain the energy's in. And when they are mixed and balanced, they come together to form Universal Life Force Energy [the Holy Spirit].

The Central Circuit is your own personal, "Holy Grail", and the "Fountain of Youth", is also within us. We may fill our own cups from within, and they may forever, overflow.

The Electromagnetic Energy we produce from combining Solar and Lunar Energy's within us, is clearly felt flowing through our tongue as it makes its way through to the pituitary gland and the brain, and flows through the Central Circuit.

The Tongue is not just the Master switch of the brain and the Central Circuit, but also acts as a kind of feedback monitor, allowing the practitioners to directly feel the strong electromagnetic flow we contain in the body's Central Circuit. It feels like electricity flowing through your tongue up into your brain, and that's exactly what's happening.

The Practitioner can control the amount of energy the body is producing, with the intensity of their muscle contractions, while practicing "The Breath of Light". Firm contractions produce a nice steady output, and strong contractions make strong energy production. Generally we use firm contractions to produce a nice gentle energy output, but if you were to want to use the energy to heal someone, we can increase our output with stronger contractions of the perineum and torso muscles, to produce a stronger flow. It's really that Simple.

The "Breath of Light" technique, is the only way I have discovered to wilfully Balance the body's Central Circuit on a daily basis, and experience,

"Enlightenment Made Manifest."

It's a very real experience of being a true co-creator, giving birth to Universal Life Force Energy's from within us, every day. And we develop an Ever-increasing, Conscious Awareness, as a result of our positive focus, on our Cultivation Practice each and every day,[until the practice is entirely natural].

We get to a point where we only need to think of raising our Kundalini up through all of our purified chakras to our crown, and it happens in an instant. Thought is faster than the speed of light. We can switch the force On and Off with a thought. We can direct the Force from one hand to the other, or anywhere we desire with our intent.

[CHAPTER TWO]

AUTHORS NOTES

This is a technique that transcends being a technique, with regular practice. It's a way of using more of our body's muscles, as we naturally breathe, to achieve and maintain the Balance of the body's internal energy systems, and allow the Kundalini to naturally rise, when balance is attained.

With its practice as a daily spiritual discipline, you can expect to experience a Living, Vibrating, Electromagnetic Force that comes from within yourself, from your centre of Light and Gravity.

You will experience an increase in Life Force Energies, felt directly flowing through your tongue at first, and through your hands quite strongly with regular practice.

The tongue and finger mudras, some people will be familiar with from yoga and meditation really come alive with the regular practice of the "The Breath of Light". They act as feedback

Monitors, allowing the practitioner to directly feel the energy's they are producing from within, as they cultivate their breaths.

This direct experience, and increased energy levels encourage the practitioner to continue on and on with their Cultivation practice. 'While the Force we Experience always remains a Great Mystery'.

There are two main paths that the Seeker comes across on the journey to Enlightenment.

"The path of Surrender and the path of Will."

On my personal journey, one led me to the other. Firstly while I experimented with meditation, I found that Surrendering Constant Thoughts, and resting my mind, in Silent observation,[observing without thinking about what I was observing], allowed me to experience Transidential consciousness, which is wonderfully liberating from the constant grind of everyday thoughts. Inner vision became apparent with colours and symbols, as I simply observed. I could also hear high frequencies. Daily Meditation has many benefits, and I can only encourage you to experiment for yourself. Everybody is unique in their own way, and our abilities often vary. One person may be a gifted visionary, while another may hear the voices of spirit guides, and it's only through practice and experimentation that we discover our strengths and weaknesses.

"But life goes on", and we must return to our everyday lives and everyday consciousness. And I found myself looking for more of the mystery and magic, experienced in higher states of consciousness [that require a state of trance to experience] in my everyday consciousness.

This is where 'the path of Will' came to my attention, and breath cultivation became my, daily spiritual discipline, about 25 years ago. I discovered I could balance the Bio-Circuitry and Energy Centres of my body, with the daily practice of "The Breath of Light".

Whatever Path in life you decide to walk, you will be <u>breathing</u> as you walk that path, and those breaths can be cultivated simultaneously, as you perform any activity at all.

After many years of practicing the 'breath of light' with every conscious breath It's become entirely natural, and there is no thought of technique anymore. It's just a way of using more of my body's muscles, to maintain the internal balance of my energy centres, as I naturally breathe.

When I'm not speaking, eating or kissing, the tip of my tongue is connected to the pituitary point [to the middle of the lump, just back from the highest part of the upper Palate], all day long.

In Tantric Teachings, this lumpy bit, is the body's inner clitoris and the tongue is the inner penis, connecting them is an act of making love to yourself, and unifying the male and female energy's within the Central Circuit.

7

As you practice the 'breath of light' you will strengthen your tongue making it easier to do the practice, and the lump you can feel, swells as it develops, receiving the electromagnetic force we cultivate, flowing through the tongue to this important Pituitary Meridian, and back into the body's Central Circuit, [your internal holy grail].

I would like to here quote, some brief passages from the wonderful book, [Jewel in the Lotus, the tantric path to higher consciousness], directly relating to the Tongue mudra.

'The tongue mudra is helpful in quieting the mind. As the Mind chatters, your tongue says the words silently in micro-movements. Immobilizing the tongue stops the chatter'.

'The tongue mudra is very beneficial for health, as there are pressure points and glands in the palate which control many functions in the body'.

'In opening the third eye, the psychic bridge must be joined, that is, a direct connection between the medulla to the third eye energy centre'. The tongue tip, touching the lump just back from the highest part of the palate, completes that connection and stimulates the pituitary gland. When the tongue touches the roof of the mouth, it stimulates the crown chakra. When the tongue goes way back and touches the soft palate, it stimulates the pineal gland. The awakened Pineal Gland secretes hormones that start dripping down through the system to revitalise your body. They call this fluid 'The Divine Nectar' or 'Living Water' and it contains serotonin, a precursor to endorphins the body's natural opiate. [If during the exercise you taste something bitter,[that may be harmful], and the practice should be stopped. It probably means that some chemical, like residual LSD, is stored in the brain].'

I would suggest you do a detox programme before you continue with the practice.

If this is interesting to you, why not grab yourself a copy of 'The jewel in the lotus' by Sunyata Saraswati and Bodhi Avinasha. The best Tantra book I have ever come across.

So with the tip of the tongue connected to the lump just back from the highest part of the upper palate, we use a firm contraction of certain muscles with the in and outward breath, to practice 'The Breath of Light'. This strengthens and develops Important Glands and muscles often weak in many people. Strengthening the glands responsible, for cell reproduction etc, can help slow the ageing process as well.

I also find that the 'Breath of Light' helps the practitioner to remain consciously aware, and maintain mental focus. It brings spiritual awareness into daily activities, using breath as a spiritual focus, instead of rosary beads etc.

<u>Solar, Static or Male energy</u> flows into the body from above through the crown chakra, and out of the base chakra, with each inward breath, unless you make an effort to retain it.

We do this by locking the base chakra, by contracting the perineum and anus muscles with each inward breath. We then fully relax these muscles as we move to the outward breath.

<u>Lunar, Magnetic or Female energy</u> flows into the body from mother earth below, through the base chakra. With each outward breath we use a wavelike contraction, that starts in the lower abdomen, and rises upwards through the torso, chest and up to the Tongue Mudra, lifting Lunar energy's into to Central Circuit, to be collected and mixed with the Solar energy so they can, come into Balance. We can clearly feel the energy's flowing through our Tongue, as we practice the tongue mudra. And just as the heart pumps and relaxes continually, we contract and relax these two different muscle groups, Alternately and Continually. This way with practice, every conscious breath may be cultivated, and utilised for our spiritual development. [If you're dedicated, and have the self- discipline required.]

[CHAPTER THREE]

'TECHNIQUE'

The 'Breath of Light' is a three step technique.

1. Tongue Mudra.

2. Perineum Contractions, with each inward breath.

3. Upward Wavelike Contraction, with each outward breath.

1. 'Tongue Mudra'. To practice the tongue mudra we place the tip of the tongue to a special pressure point on the roof of our mouth. We place the tip of our tongue, to the middle of the lump you can feel just back from the highest part of the upper palate.

   Placing the tip of your tongue here, does a number of things. Firstly it directs cultivated energy straight to the pituitary gland, making it stronger. This is the gland that tells all the other glands in the body what to do.

Strengthening this gland improves cell reproduction, and slows the ageing process.

It also drives fresh energy into the brain with each and every breath of light. This awakens sleeping brain cells by directly stimulating them with life force energy.

Secondly, it switches ON the body's most important internal Bio-Circuit, The Central Circuit. This is a circular circuit that flows through the centre of our body's, and moves through all of the body's energy centres.

In men, the circuit flows down the back of the body and up the front of our body, and in women it flows the opposite way, down the front of the body and up the back. When you practice the tongue mudra, you are connecting the "functional" or "Yin" channel, and the "Governor meridians" or "Yang" channel, well known in acupuncture, and joining them to create a circular circuit [Central Circuit], to cultivate and balance the energy's we mix and combine within us as we practice the 'Breath of Light'.

2. 'Perineum Contractions with each inward breath.'

Here we use a firm contraction, of the perineum area as we take each inward breath. This temporally, locks the base chakra, and stops the loss of Solar energy's flowing out of our body's as we naturally breath inwards, and retains it inside the "Central Circuit".

Solar energy enters the body through the crown chakra, and flows straight out the base chakra unless we make the effort to lock the base chakra, with each inward breath. We Cultivate Solar and Lunar energy's within us, to attain their true Balance, with the 'Breath of Light' practice.

It is important to remember that you must totally relax the perineum muscles as you take each outward breath.

We learn how to contract and relax these two different muscle groups, with each in and outward breath, as we naturally breathe.

3. 'Upward wavelike abdominal and torso contractions, with each outward breath.'

This is where we draw Lunar energy's up into the central circuit, to be cultivated with Solar energy's and bring them into Balance.

When you Balance the Central Circuit, all of the body's energy centres are also Balanced.

AND BALANCE IS THE KEY TO ENLIGHTENMENT AND RAISING KUNDALINI, BY OUR OWN WILL AND DOING!.

Practice, attaining and maintaining balance, using 'The Art of Cultivated Breath.'

At first it's a Spiritual Discipline, requiring a certain amount of dedication to succeed. But with 'regular practice', it can become an entirely natural way of breathing using more of the body's muscles, to attain and maintain balance, as we naturally breathe.

No matter what path in Life you decide to walk, you will be breathing as you walk that path, and those breaths can be cultivated simultaneously as you perform any activity at all.

In fact with regular practice, every conscious breath may be cultivated, as you practice the 'Breath of Light', with any activity at all.

That being said, at first you may choose to add the 'Breath of Light' to your meditation practice, and experiment for yourself with it at your own pace. We learn from the direct experience, of energy's we feel flowing within us as we practice the 'Breath of Light'.

Practice at your own natural pace of breath, as there is no need to push too hard, you will achieve balance, as long as you are dedicated, to your cultivation practice. This takes more or less time, depending on how out of balance you are, and how dedicated you are to the practice of the 'Breath of Light'.

With this practice, any traumas stored in the energy centres or body, will come to your attention, to be acknowledged and released, through the process of observation, forgiveness and consciously letting go of it.

We need to clear the body, of any blockages or traumas stored internally, so we can raise the Kundalini safely, and experience our potential, on a daily basis.

STEP 1.
'TONGUE MUDRA, TECHNIQUE'

The Tongue is the 'Master Switch' for the most important Bio-Circuit in the human body. It connects the 'Functional' or yin meridian [energy channel] and the 'Governor' or Yang Meridian [energy channel] known in acupuncture, to create a circular circuit that flows through all of the body's chakras [energy centres].

Many people with spend their entire life disconnected and will only experience 5% of their true potential, spiritually.

They will not switch On, the body's 'Central Circuit' even once wilfully, or experience the effect of being truly balanced.

So the first step to practicing the 'Breath of Light' is to check that the Tongue is Switched On, activating the Central Circuit, which we will use to cultivate solar and lunar energy within, and attain Balance.

And we do this, by placing the tip of our tongue to the roof of our mouth, to the middle of the lump you can feel just back from the highest part of the upper palate.

In Tantra this point is the inner clitoris of our body's, and the tongue is the inner penis. And when they are joined, male and female energy's can be balanced within us, and with their unity and balance, Universal Life Force Energy is Born Within us, from our centre of Light and Gravity, from our Corestar. Kundalini rises as a direct result of the harmony of opposites, through their true balance.

So the tongue is the Master Switch of the Human Body, and it's Bio-Circuitry. You will feel Electromagnetic Energy flowing through your tongue and hands quite strongly with practice, as you strengthen this very special Circuit.

The tongue acts as a kind of feedback monitor, as well. It allows us to directly feel the flow of life force moving within us as we cultivate. This is reassuring for the practitioner, and encourages us to continue on and on with our 'Breath of Light' practice.

The Electromagnetic Universal Life Force Energy which we learn to create from within ourselves, is felt in the tongue as a kind of electrical tingling, and sometimes can feel like a cool soothing feeling, as we balance the Solar [male] and Lunar [female] energy's within the central circuit.

So this is the first of the three main steps of the 'Breath of Light'. We use these three actions, to control the circulation and flow of Solar and Lunar energy's inside the body's Bio-Circuitry, as we naturally breathe.

Our Goal, is to attain and maintain, the balance of Solar and Lunar energy's within the body's Bio-Circuitry, on a daily basis, allowing spontaneous Enlightenment to occur.

We direct energy's through the Pineal and pituitary glands, and through the brain, making them stronger with each and every cultivated breath. This awakens dormant brain cells, and allows us to tap into the other 95% of our potential, spiritually and energetically.

The second step of the 'Breath of Light' is to contract the perineum area, with each inward breath. Then totally relax it with the outward breath.

The third step to the 'Breath of Light' is to make an upward wavelike contraction from the lower Abdominal area, up through the Torso and chest and up to the tongue mudra, with each outward breath.

In the coming pages, I will give reason for the second and third steps of the 'Breath of Light'.

At first, this may seem like allot to take in, but when put into practice it's really quite simple to practice.

STEP 2.
'PERINEUM CONTRACTIONS'

The second step to the 'Breath of Light' is the Perineum Contractions, with each inward breath. This actually locks the base chakra temporarily, and allows us to hold on to Solar energy usually lost with each breath, and redirect its flow within the body's Bio-Circuitry for cultivation with lunar energy within the Central Circuit.

So we contract the perineum with each inward breath, and at the same time, make sure our belly and torsos etc. are totally relaxed until the outward breath. Just like a young child naturally breaths, our belly goes in and out like a pump, or bellows for your body's internal fire.

We then relax the perineum totally as we make the outward breath, and use a wavelike contraction from the lower Abdomen up through the Torso and chest to our tongue.

With the alternate contraction and relaxation of these two different muscle groups, and with the tongue mudra in position, we draw Solar and Lunar energy's into the body from above through the crown chakra, and below through the base chakra, into the body's Central Circuit to be combined and balanced.

Balancing the body's Central Circuit, brings balance to all of the body's energy centres. It flows right through the centre of all of them.

With the attainment of true balance of the body's energy system, Enlightenment is a natural spontaneous state of being. Although the experience of Enlightenment may vary and differ from person to person, in accord with our natural inherent, abilities.

So in summary, of the second step of the 'Breath of Light.'

We hold the perineum contraction, which locks the base chakra, and holds on to the Solar energy otherwise lost with each and every inward breath. This energy is then redirected up into the body's central circuit, for cultivation.

The 'Breath of Light' is a form of internal Alchemy. We learn how to balance male and female energy's, within us and create universal Life Force Energy [Kundalini], from our centre of Light and Gravity.

We can raise this energy up through our purified energy centres, and it flows out of our heart and crown chakras, just like a fountain. We can control this energy with our mental intention, switching it on and off with a thought, once balance is attained and maintained.

'Your body is a Holy Grail, and the fountain of youth is within you. You can fill your own cup from within, and it may forever overflow.'

With balance, Life Force is born within us, and we give it out in all directions, just like a Star.

This is the hidden potential of all human beings, to become a true co-creator, and give life force energy to all that surrounds us, and be continually, 'Enlightened'.

STEP 3.
<u>'UPWARD WAVELIKE TORSO</u> <u>CONTRACTIONS'</u>

'Pumping the bellows of the internal fire'

This is the third step of the 'Breath of Light' practice.

With each outward breath, we use a wavelike contraction, which moves in an upward manner, from the lower abdomen, up through the Torso and chest, delivering energy's to the Tongue Mudra.

This wavelike contraction, acts like a bellow for our internal fire. It's the pumping driving force, of our cultivation practice, circulating energy's around the body's central circuit.

As we relax the perineum muscles, after the inward breath, this wavelike contraction raises Lunar Energy up through the base chakra to be mixed with the Solar Energy retained with the inward breath.

The contraction and relaxation of these two different muscle groups, and with the tongue tip to the pituitary point, we cause an internal alchemy to take place. When solar and lunar energy's are perfectly balanced, within the body's 'Central Circuit', 'Magic really happens'. Our natural potential comes into being, and Enlightenment is spontaneous. We produce Universal Life Force Energy's from our centre of Light and gravity, as long as we maintain balance with the practice of the 'Breath of Light', there is no limit to the amount of Life Force we can produce.

There is a lot of interest in free energy devices, around the world. But so few people realise, that this is their own hidden potential. And all that is required to experience this for yourself, is to balance your body's energy systems.

"We can be true co-creators of Life Force, and Bio-Photonic Light, and give without limit, every day of our lives."

Is that not worth the effort required to master the 'Breath of Light?'

<u>In the Final Summary, of the three main steps, of the 'Breath of Light'.</u>

The Primary Goal of the 'Breath of Light' practice is to bring balance to the Solar and Lunar energy's we cultivate inside the body's Central Circuit. When balance is attained, we create Universal Life Force Energy from their unity, which leaves the body as Electromagnetic Energy.

It takes great discipline to Master the 'Breath of Light', but anyone can do it. Persevere with your 'Breath of Light' practice, and you will achieve balance and experience much more of your natural potential.

BALANCE = ENLIGHTENMENT

You may at first choose to practice the 'Breath of Light' with your meditation in the morning or evening. But I suggest that you build on that, at your own pace and speed. Increasing the regularity of your Cultivation Practice, and integrating it into your daily activities.

This brings Spiritual Awareness into daily activities, as well as helping us to remain consciously aware throughout the day.

Eventually you will find that every conscious breath can be cultivated and utilized for your spiritual development, and well being.

Just like everything in life, 'you will only get out of it what you put into it'. And just as the heart pumps and relaxes, but never stops, so it can be with the 'Breath of Light' practice.

I am at your service, if you have any questions, I will endeavour to answer them for you, if it is within my abilities at the time.

NOTE: If you feel a hot flushing feeling at your base chakra, or a tingling through your feet. You have probably disconnected your tongue mudra, or failed to contract the perineum, firmly enough, with the inward breath.

Just check your technique, and keep on practicing.

Every cultivated breath is an opportunity to raise your vibrational level, breath by breath, step by step. Its an opportunity to heal yourself, as prana [universal life force energy] is the best medicine.

BEFOR ENLIGHTENMENT, CART WATER AND CHOP WOOD.

AFTER ENLIGHTENMENT, CART WATER AND CHOP WOOD.

[Old Chinese saying.]

'ABOUT THE AUTHOR'

Everybody has certain, inherent natural abilities. One person may be gifted in mathematics, while another has a gift for cooking.

I have been gifted with visionary abilities all of my life. That is to say I have had a number of visions throughout my life. As I have spiritually evolved, I have had a number of initiations that involved profound visions, and physical experiences that have been life changing.

As a boy, one day I was lying on the floor, relaxed listening to music, when suddenly I had my first vision. My third eye opened, and I could see a spinning wheel before me, it had different sections, like spokes on a wheel, and in each section of the wheel, it appeared that there were movies of different parts of my life, from childhood through to adulthood. I could also journey into each section of the wheel viewing what was going on, and come out again, to see the wheel of my Life spinning before me.

The experience came to an end, and I found myself back in my body. But I could only remember the sections of the wheel before my present age, for same reason I was not allowed to see my future.

I have ever since known there is much more to our reality, than what meets the eyes.

Another profound experience happened when I was at High School. I had gone to visit a good friend at his girlfriend's house, on the weekend. It was in the morning and I was lying down meditating. My mate came into the room, and saw me meditating and said, don't let me disturb you, I will press some pressure points my martial arts teacher showed me and I'll leave the room. I did not even open my eyes and carried on meditating, as he pressed some points on the left side of my body, and left the room.

Suddenly I could feel a Powerful energy flowing into my body, from my hands and feet, it came up to my heart chakra and exploded out of my heart centre. It was so powerful it was causing me to arch upward from the bed.

At the same time, I was having a vision. As the energy's moved through my body. I could see a temple just like the Taj Mahal in India, in my inner vision. I could see colourful energy's rushing through and around the Temple, as I had the experience. After about half a hour of this wonderful experience, things returned to normal.

I found my friend in the next room, and asked him what he did to me? He just smiled and said, 'We just have a special connection, mate. It's something my martial arts teacher showed me.' I am forever grateful for this heart opening experience, my dear friend 'Gregory Uppington'.

I hope that by sharing these experiences, it is of some use in understanding me.

The next most profound spiritual experience that changed my life, was in my teens. I took a friend into the mountains behind Brisbane. He was a tourist from England, and I was taking him to see the rainforest, and wonderful big trees I know that have cave like holes which you can climb inside and up into the trees. They are huge Fig trees, in the rainforest. After visiting these special trees, we went to a lookout, to see the setting Sun.

I decided to lie down, and meditate, when my friend said would you mind if I 'speak in tongue', as you meditate, I said go ahead, and continued to meditate.

Well as he spoke in tongue, which I had never heard before, I could understand what he was saying, to my surprise. He was asking for the 'Holy Spirit', of the one true God to come through my body, as I meditated.

Suddenly Energy started rushing from the centre of my body, outwards in all directions. It flowed out from my hands and feet, and out of my head like a fountain, it was the most wonderful, powerful, tingling, rushing experience of Energy I had ever experienced in my Life.

I was feeling this energetic experience, while at the same time, I was having a vision.

I could see a royal blue triangle in my inner vision and inside the triangle was the golden 'Eye of Horus'. The experience lasted for about an hour, after the vision part of the experience, it was just the experience of energy rushing from my body, which slowly dissipated.

It was a wonderful experience, and it showed me what amazing potential we all have, and just how much energy we can have flowing through us all the time.

Our potential is truly amazing, and just as they say we are only using 5% of our brain, I'd say it's the same with our Energetic output level. We are much more powerful than most people ever realise, and all that is required to experience this for ourselves, is to Balance the body's energy centres, and Central Bio-Circuitry.

So there I was at the lookout, filled with wonderment once again, from the most profound experience I had ever had in my life before, buzzing with energy. I looked at my friend and said 'What was that?' He smiled, and said he had had a similar experience, in the jungles of far north Queensland, with an Aboriginal Elder, and that the Elder also told him, one day he would pass this experience on to another, and that that person turned out to be me. He also said that I should check out the Bible as there were some answers to be found inside.

Well years went by, and I searched to try and find out how I could reproduce the experience of the Holy Spirit, of my own will and doing. I was studying two different schools of thought, Taoism and Tantra [Kriya or Kundalini Yoga].

I learned about the tongue mudras, and the micro-cosmic circuit,[Circular, Central Circuit], within the human body, and I just knew I was on to something.

One Day I was walking along experimenting with a breathing exercise I created, with some key points I had learned from these two different schools of thought, when the magic happened, and I balanced my energy centres, by the continual practice of this breathing method, and the "Holy Spirit experience" returned to me, by my own will and doing.

Well this was better than winning the lottery to me, everything, just fell into place and the 'Breath of Light' was born.

'The Breath of Light' unlocked the hidden potential within me, and allowed me to produce the 'Holy Spirit' [Kundalini, or Universal Life Force Energy] from within my, Core Star [centre of Light and Gravity].

If you are dedicated to your "Breath of Light" practice, you will unlock your own hidden potential.

You can create unlimited amounts of Life Force, from within yourself, and be a true co-creator of Life Force and Bio-Photonic Light.

Now that has got to be worth the dedication required to Master, the 'Breath of Light'.